**Peggy Guggenheim's
Other Legacy**

Peggy Guggenheim's Other Legacy

Curated by Melvin P. Lader
and Fred Licht

The exhibition is made possible
by a generous grant from
The Bankers Trust Company Group

New York, March - May 1987
Solomon R. Guggenheim Museum

Venice, October 1987 - January 1988
Peggy Guggenheim Collection

Managing Editor
Maria Cristina Poma

Executive Editor
Alessandra Sacchi

Editorial Staff Members
Antonella Minetto
Valeria Sperti

Secretarial Staff
Manuela Oggioni
Anna Romanelli

Art Director
FG Confalonieri

Technical Bureau
Studio g.due srl

ISBN 88-04-30090-6

Contents

Peggy Guggenheim at her
desk in Palazzo Venier
dei Leoni, Venice.
Photograph courtesy of the
Estate of Roloff Beny.

Preface and acknowledgments

The title of this exhibition, Peggy Guggenheim's Other Legacy, *refers to works that have either been owned or have been shown by our collector patron but are not now in the possession of The Solomon R. Guggenheim Foundation and its Venetian museum. This is unfortunate or fortunate, depending upon the contrary perspectives of those who presently either lack or possess the art in question. What is indisputable, however, is that these nearly sixty paintings, sculptures and works on paper were sufficiently important to Peggy for her either to acquire them or at least to incorporate them in one of her numerous exhibitions held between the fall of 1942 and the spring of 1947 at her New York gallery-museum, "Art of This Century".*

Peggy Guggenheim's Other Legacy, *therefore, should have the effect of introducing those unfamiliar with Peggy's collecting effort to a normally hidden dimension while at the same time broadening the view of those whose information is limited to the Collection's annual showing at the Palazzo Venier dei Leoni in Venice. For the latter the acquaintance with artists that were within the collector's scope without now being represented among her Venetian holdings will no doubt be informative. But the deepening that results from a mental tally, whereby works selected for this exhibition are added to familiar examples in Venice, will lead to an even greater enrichment and an enhanced comprehension of Peggy's aims and achievements.*

Since the works of art needed for the illumination of Peggy Guggenheim's intentions as a collector have now for many years been dispersed throughout the world, a conscientious search preceded loan requests addressed to private and institutional owners. The exhibition is, among other things, a testimony to the generosity with which such requests were received, and our first expression of gratitude therefore is directed toward lenders separately listed in the pages of this catalogue and including those who preferred to remain anonymous.

The proposal to search out and present, in exhibition form, collection items that Peggy had given during her lifetime to museums other than her own, came to us from Professor Fred Licht before he was appointed Curator of the Peggy Guggenheim Collection in Venice. Subsequently Professor Melvin P. Lader approached us with a project that would concentrate upon Peggy's activities at "Art of This Century". This exhibition is therefore a composite of two, originally separate notions. Each of the originators has assumed curatorial responsibility for the subject of his particular interest. Our thanks therefore are herewith addressed to the two co-curators, and to Susan B. Hirschfeld who acted as coordinator of the show. Although Peggy Guggenheim's Other Legacy *is a project of the Peggy Guggenheim Collection, its first showing is at the Solomon R. Guggenheim Museum where Ann Kraft, the Museum's Executive Associate, maintains contact between the Guggenheim Foundation's two operating branches. Her liaison work as applied to this exhibition as well as the distinct contributions of Philip Rylands, Deputy Director of the Peggy Guggenheim Collection, and the efforts of his staff are herewith acknowledged.*

Finally, but not without awareness of its crucial importance, I wish to express the Foundation's profound gratitude to The Bankers Trust Company Group without whose generous grant this exhibition could not have been presented in New York.

Thomas M. Messer, Director
The Solomon R. Guggenheim Foundation

Berenice Abbott/Commerce
Graphics Ltd. Inc.,
"Surrealist Gallery, Art of This
Century", 1942.
Photograph courtesy of
Mrs. Lillian Kiesler.

Peggy Guggenheim's "Art of This Century"

In 1941, when World War II made it dangerous for Peggy Guggenheim to remain any longer in Europe, she returned to the United States, bringing with her not only an already celebrated collection of modern art but, less tangibly, an adventurous spirit that had surfaced early in her life and which she had sustained while living abroad since 1920 among avant-garde artists, writers, musicians, performers and kindred creative personalities. Among her friends and acquaintances in pre-war Europe were such important figures of the modern art world as Marcel Duchamp, André Breton, Piet Mondrian, Yves Tanguy and Max Ernst, to note a few. Peggy, as she liked to be called, was encouraged by her friends to make modern art her destiny. Starting in the 1930s, she collected works by Arp, Brancusi, Kandinsky, and Moore, which whetted her appetite for collecting the even more daringly advanced art of her Surrealist milieu in Europe. Stimulated by finding herself a stranger in the country of her birth, she opened "Art of This Century" at 30 West 57th Street in New York in 1942 and proceeded to show the most audacious American art to a still hesitant public.

"Art of This Century" was not Peggy Guggenheim's first experience in directing a gallery, for she had opened another gallery, "Guggenheim Jeune", in London in 1938. That establishment quickly earned a reputation as a showplace for modern art, especially Surrealism, and some of the group and one-man exhibitions that Peggy sponsored there were prototypes for those seen at "Art of This Century" later on. "Guggenheim Jeune" effectively tested conservative British taste and challenged the public to respond to new and unfamiliar art, a *modus operandi* she was to use in America as well. Although "Guggenheim Jeune" was a financial failure there evolved from it the idea of opening a museum of modern art in England to house her rapidly growing art collection. These plans for a museum were cut short, however, by Hitler's menacing presence, and America fell heir to them. After returning to the United States, Peggy Guggenheim searched for a suitable location for her museum, seriously considering San Francisco and New Orleans before finally deciding on New York. Such searching beyond the East coast reflected her desire to introduce modern art to places relatively unexposed to it, just as she was later to donate works to out-of-the-way museums. San Francisco, for example, was ruled out because Peggy did not wish to duplicate the efforts of the San Francisco Museum of Art, directed by Dr. Grace McCann Morley[1], with whom she remained in close touch during her stay in America.

Perhaps sensing the excitement brewing among artists in New York, but more likely influenced by the fact that many of her friends and acquaintances from Europe had settled there for the duration of the War, Peggy selected New York as the site for her museum. She did so despite the fact that it already had The Museum of Modern Art, directed by Alfred H. Barr, Jr. (who became an ally of Peggy's in the crusade for modernism), The Whitney Museum of American Art, and the Museum of Non-Objective Painting (now the Solomon R. Guggenheim Museum), where Peggy's uncle exhibited an impressive array of modern European painting as well as sculpture. Peggy incorporated into her plans for the new museum a commercial gallery through which she could exhibit contemporary European and American art. "Art of This Century" thus became the only 57th Street gallery of the period to show European moderns and simultaneously to risk introducing new American artists.

To reflect the aesthetic orientation of the museum-gallery, Peggy hired the innovative architect, Frederick Kiesler, to design a fitting environment. He divided the space into four galleries: one devoted to the permanent collection of Cubist and abstract works; a second and third devoted to the Surrealist works; and a fourth reserved for the gallery's changing exhibitions. With the exception of the gallery for temporary shows, Kiesler designed the galleries in a manner reflecting the styles of art they were to contain. Thus the Surrealist gallery with its concavely curved walls, dramatic lighting and unframed pictures mounted on special wooden arms projecting from the walls, created an appropriately unsettling environment. The Cubist gallery on the other hand seemed more rational, with its cool fluorescent lighting and a quasi-geometric system of ropes and wooden wedges to support the unframed paintings and sculptures. The objects from the permanent collection thus displayed served as historical background and as an aesthetic basis for the individual and group shows in the commercial gallery, silently stressing the continuity between the earlier modern styles and the new art.

The primary purpose of the gallery was clearly recorded in a press release issued at the time of the gallery's opening in October of 1942. In it, Peggy Guggenheim stated her hope that "Art of This Century" would "become a center where artists will be welcome and where they can feel that they are cooperating in establishing a research laboratory for new ideas", a statement that underscores her compulsive desire for change, experimentation and innovation. She continued, "This undertaking will serve only if it succeeds in serving the future instead of recording the past"[2].

Over the five years of "Art of This Century's" existence, three types of exhibitions were held: group shows, one-man exhibitions and those shows organized around a particular theme. New talents were usually introduced in group shows, such as the *Exhibition of Collage* (1943), the two *Spring Salons* (1943 and 1944), or the *Autumn Salon* (1945). A promising artist introduced in this way was often granted a solo exhibition soon thereafter. Of the forty one-man shows at "Art of This Century", more than half were given to new American artists, while the balance consisted of European moderns like Jean Arp, Giorgio de Chirico, Alberto Giacometti, Theo van Doesburg, Jean Hélion and Pablo Picasso. Thematic shows on the other hand were also innovative, with two exhibitions devoted to the art of women; one to the relationship between natural, insane and Surrealist art; an exhibition featuring some paintings never before seen in America; and a show comparing the early and late works of fifteen modern artists.

The opening of "Art of This Century" elicited a great deal of critical attention, which dwelt as much on Kiesler's spectacular architectural design as on the paintings and sculptures. The permanent collection did indeed establish the general modernist and avant-garde tenor of the gallery and aptly set the stage for the first exhibition season, during which shows devoted to Surrealism and abstract art were augmented by the introduction of some new names. Although paintings by de Chirico, Duchamp, Braque, Ernst, Kandinsky, Mirò, Mondrian and Picasso were the rule, works by Baziotes, Motherwell, Pollock, Hare, Kamrowksi, Lassaw and de Kooning also appeared for the first time.

It was at the *Exhibition of Collage* in April 1943, the first of its type ever mounted in America, that many of the future stars of the gallery were first represented. The exhibition was based upon a similar show Peggy had done at "Guggenheim Jeune" in 1938, and the decision to open up the show to American artists was in keeping with the gallery's philosophy of showing new talent. Alongside European collages were some of the first works by such "unknowns" as Baziotes, Motherwell, Kamrowski and Pollock, all of whom Peggy encouraged to participate. Not only was it a welcome opportunity for them to exhibit, but the fact that they were in such distinguished company made the opportunity all the more important. The show held further significance for both Baziotes and Motherwell, who realized their first sales when the Baltimore collector, Saidie May, purchased Baziotes' *The Drugged Balloonist* (1943) and Motherwell's *The Joy of Living* (1943) from the gallery. Kamrowski's *Untitled* (1942), which is included in the present exhibition, proved that American artists were experimenting effectively with Surrealist techniques and imagery. Motherwell of course went on to explore the collage medium extensively after this first experimentation.

Immediately following the collage show, "Art of This Century" presented another milestone exhibition in the first of three Salon exhibitions, the purpose of which was to present the work of young talented artists, who otherwise had had little exposure. The concept of a seasonal Salon was borrowed from the French system and was suggested by Herbert Read for use at "Guggenheim Jeune". No Salon was ever held at the London gallery but Peggy who remembered the idea implemented it later at "Art of This Century" in May-June of 1943, where a jury of six (Marcel Duchamp, Piet Mondrian, James Johnson Sweeney, James Thrall Soby, Howard Putzel and Peggy Guggenheim) accepted forty-three works for the exhibition, including two versions of *The Mirror at Midnight* by Baziotes, *Pancho Villa Dead and Alive* by Motherwell and *Stenographic Figure* by Pollock.

Pollock's painting in the first *Spring Salon* left the jury "starry-eyed"[3]. His unconventional style of painting soon stirred Peggy's enthusiasm (though she was admittedly a little hesitant at first), and he became her chief protégé by late spring. In fact Pollock was the only artist to whom Guggenheim ever offered a contract with the gallery. After his appearances in the collage show and the *Spring Salon*, she made plans for the first of his four one-man shows at "Art of This Century" early in the second season (November 9-27, 1943).

Pollock created several of his key paintings for that important show, among them being *Male and Female, Guardians of the Secret, The Moon Woman Cuts the Circle,* and *The She-Wolf.* Peggy perceptively assessed the show as "something of an event in the contemporary history of American art" and described the artist as one of "the strongest and most interesting American painters"[4]. Sweeney, who was on the Advisory Committee of The Museum of Modern Art, wrote a foreword to the catalogue in which his enthusiasm captured the spirit of Pollock's style: "Pollock's talent is volcanic. It has fire. It is unpredictable. It is undisciplined. It spills itself out in a mineral prodigality not yet crystallized. It is lavish, explosive, untidy"[5].

Critical response to Pollock's first show was plentiful, with several reviewers noting his special promise for American art. Clement Greenberg, who was himself a newcomer to the art community, praised Pollock's intense, dark, murky colors that approximated the moods created by native writers such as Edgar Allan Poe, Herman Melville and Nathaniel Hawthorne[6]. A review by Robert Motherwell, the artist's colleague, is revealing also, for in it he spoke of Pollock as one of a handful of a young generation of painters who had a real chance to succeed. Despite Pollock's wealth of talent, his chances for success might have been greatly reduced or delayed without Peggy Guggenheim's support.

Peggy organized second, third and fourth one-man shows for Pollock in 1945, 1946 and 1947. Virtually every major early work by him including the magnificent *Mural* (1943) was painted in preparation for these shows and made its debut at the gallery. A number of examples in the current exhibition attest to the historical importance of these shows and to Peggy Guggenheim's faith in Pollock's talent when few dealers would have even recognized it. Ironically, in view of Pollock's role as a leader of Abstract Expressionism, comparatively few sales of his work were effected through "Art of This Century" - only thirty-two works were sold during a period of five years[7]. Pollock's exhibition was the first of many historical one-man shows for which "Art of This Century" became known. During the second season, oils, gouaches and drawings by the German émigré Hans Hofmann were presented. Considerably older than the other artists who would become central figures of Abstract Expressionism, Hofmann differed from them also in having had a number of exhibitions previously and having achieved considerable fame as an art teacher. However, his show at "Art of This Century" featured his most spontaneous and improvisational works of c. 1943-1944 such as the untitled gouache now in the Tel Aviv Museum[8]. The critics spoke of Hofmann's paintings as being virtually non-objective, though they also noted the presence of some lyrical landscape paintings and several other canvases with grotesque symbols[9]. It was during the second season, too, that works by Pollock, Motherwell, Alexander Calder and Joseph Cornell were seen with those of the European Surrealists in the *Natural, Insane, Surrealist Art* exhibition in December 1943, while David Hare's *The Frog is a Heart* and Mark Rothko's *The Entombment* joined Pollock's *Pasiphae* in *First Exhibition in America of (Twenty Paintings)* in April of the following year. The final show of that season was the second *Spring Salon for Young Artists* in which Baziotes, Motherwell, Pollock and Hare were once again represented, now in the company of works by

Richard Pousette-Dart and eighteen others. Here Baziotes exhibited his breakthrough painting, *The Balcony*, which he had painted early in 1944. The 1944-1945 season was the gallery's most important one, for that year Peggy enthusiastically granted one-man shows to Baziotes, Motherwell, Hare and Rothko in addition to presenting Pollock's second show as noted earlier. In each case, the formative work by these new artists drew the attention of the critics and public alike, who if not totally sympathetic to the newly emerging Abstract Expressionist aesthetic, often at least sensed these artists' potential. Peggy Guggenheim herself continued to emphasize her role and that of the gallery in presenting young experimental art, as evidenced by the press release issued on the occasion of Baziotes' show: "This consistent endeavor [to introduce new talents] is being continued with the exhibition of the work by a young man whose serious search and experimentation establishes him as a potentially potent force in the progress of creative art"[10]. At other times, Peggy stressed the innovative nature of the art or the theory of the painter or sculptor in an attempt to explain or clarify the artists' works. She therefore spoke of Baziotes' ability to instill mystery in color and form, and Motherwell's sensitivity for his medium and his talent for authentically deriving from nature a vocabulary of abstract forms that he could adapt to it. David Hare, a photographer-turned-sculptor, was highlighted as a determined youth who had sacrificed a promising career in color photography to experiment with a medium in which he could better realize his aspirations to communicate. Lastly, she identified Rothko's art as representing the new, emerging style of painting, stressing the difficulty in classifying it and noting its strong ties to both abstraction and Surrealism. The press release also spoke of Rothko's archaizing quality, his mythic style and his evocative forms and space that fused the historical conscious and subconscious.

It could be argued that the "Art of This Century" press releases functioned as effective teaching tools. As so many of her friends have pointed out, Peggy Guggenheim was both an avid student of art and an eager teacher, despite her efforts to appear naïve and bohemian. It is of little importance whether or not she actually wrote the press releases (few of them bear the stamp of her writing style); what does matter is that she undoubtedly gave her approval before they were issued to the newspapers and magazines.

Some of the critics responded directly to the press releases. Greenberg praised Peggy Guggenheim's enterprise in presenting shows by new artists, and complimented her on her eye for quality. "Two of the abstract painters she has recently introduced – Jackson Pollock and William Baziotes – reveal more than promise: on the strength of their one-man shows they have already placed themselves among the six or seven best young painters we possess"[11]. Critic Jon Stroup spoke of Motherwell's "enjoyment of the materials of his medium" and the degree to which "subject matter and medium govern form"[12], while Maude Riley wrote a lengthy review on the elusiveness of Rothko's style and his mythological subjects[13]. An anonymous review that was published in *Art News* perceptively noted the quiet effect produced by Rothko's color and paint, contrasted with the intricate, powerful imagery[14]. David Hare's potential as a sculptor was cleverly verbalized by Riley in another of her reviews, "The hare has become the hunter and David seems on the track of something worth overtaking"[15].

The 1945-1946 exhibition season at the gallery continued the feverish pace of innovative shows. Supplementing the *Spring Salons*, Peggy initiated an *Autumn Salon* in October, in which works by most of the artists she had introduced earlier appeared (Hare, Kamrowski, Motherwell, Pollock, Pousette-Dart and Rothko). There were, however, some additional names that would become familiar in the context of Abstract Expressionism: Clyfford Still, Willem de Kooning, Adolph Gottlieb and Charles Seliger. This was the only time that de Kooning (represented by *The Wave*) and Gottlieb participated in "Art of This Century", unlike Still and Seliger who soon had one-man shows there. Both de Kooning and Gottlieb had been offered one-man shows, however, when Howard Putzel, who had a keen eye for talent and was instrumental in persuading Guggenheim to take on some of these artists, was serving as secretary to the gallery. But de Kooning declined because he did not think he was ready for such an exhibition, and Gottlieb evidently preferred to show with Putzel after he left Peggy's employ in 1944 and opened his own "67 Gallery".

Charles Seliger was the youngest of all the painters involved in the American avant-garde of the 1940s. When he had his first exhibition at "Art of This Century" in November 1945, he was only nineteen years old, but already a familiar figure on the art scene in New York. Among the thirteen paintings and numerous drawings and "objects" Seliger exhibited were his *Cerebral Landscape* and *Don Quixote* (both dated 1944), the latter being singled out by critic Judith Kaye Reed as one of his outstanding pieces. The organic and visceral qualities in his paintings placed him firmly in the Surrealist tradition, while his personal adaptation of automatism related him to many young Americans who were also experimenting with the technique. Jon Stroup authored the foreword to Seliger's catalogue, in which he defined the artist's work "as an apotheosis of viscera, contrapuntally punctuated with the image of the phallus", a definition that was quoted frequently in other reviews[16]. Seliger has never been fully absorbed into the history of Abstract Expressionism, largely because his art developed along a similar but independent course, preserving a more meditated (i.e. less spontaneous) process and a more intimate scale.

It was Rothko who was responsible for bringing the West coast painter Clyfford Still to Peggy Guggenheim's attention in 1945. Still's inclusion in the *Autumn Salon* was followed four months later by his one-man show (February-March 1946). In Rothko's foreword to the catalogue, he pointed out the similarity between Still's canvases and those of other painters in New York who were exploring mythical content. Fourteen paintings were included in the exhibition, including the well-known *Self-Portrait* which is now in the San Francisco Museum of Art, and *Jamais* which is in the Peggy Guggenheim Collection in Venice. All of Still's paintings that were shown at "Art of This Century" were quite large in scale – the largest exhibited until then at "Art of This Century" – and may well have reinforced the tendency

towards grand size in the work of Pollock and other American artists in the late 1940s.

Rounding out the third season of exhibitions, there were additional shows for David Hare (his second of three; January-February 1946) and for Pollock. This proved to be Hare's most successful show in terms of critical attention. Among the twenty-three sculptures shown were his key works, *The Magician's Game*, *Young Girl* and *The Couple*. His spiritual affinity to Surrealism was noted by nearly every reviewer, as was the relationship of his work in its attenuated form and macabre humor to those of Giacometti. Clement Greenberg, who earlier had singled out Jackson Pollock as the most gifted American young painter[17], now assessed Hare's talent similarly as being second only to David Smith as a sculptor of artistic potential[18].

Somewhat of an anomaly among the shows of 1945-1946 was one given to paintings by Janet Sobel (January 1946). She had previously exhibited in the second of two shows devoted to women artists. An untrained painter, Sobel's early style was primitive, based largely upon personal experiences or upon her Russian Jewish heritage. Her naïve way of painting had prompted Sidney Janis to include her in his book *They Taught Themselves* and later in the 1944 exhibition *Abstract and Surrealist Art in the United States* that toured the country in 1944. By 1946, Sobel had generally abandoned her primitive, representational manner of painting for a more abstract, all-over style in which facial features or other images often evolved from a web of linear rhythms. Works like *Milky Way* (which was in her show at "Art of This Century") were commented upon for their abstract qualities and their kinship to Surrealist automatism. It was evidently this aspect of Sobel's art that appealed to Peggy Guggenheim and prompted her to schedule Sobel's exhibition.

Richard Pousette-Dart was the only major young artist to have a first one-man show at "Art of This Century" during the last exhibition season, 1946-1947, though Pollock and Hare, of course, also had solo shows. Although Pousette-Dart had been represented twice earlier in group shows at Peggy's gallery, he had been exhibiting primarily at Marian Willard's gallery through 1946. His show at "Art of This Century" in March 1947 resulted from Peggy's enthusiasm for his work and, in part, the large size of his canvases, which required more extensive exhibition space. In paintings such as *Symphony no. 1: The Transcendental* and *Comprehension of the Atom, Crucifixion*, the artist tried "to express the spiritual nature of the universe", which reflected his philosophy that painting "is mysterious and transcending, yet solid and real"[19]. The canvases shown at Peggy Guggenheim's gallery were essential to the formation of Pousette-Dart's theory and style of painting and once more underscore the historical importance of these exhibitions. The abstractly expressed spiritual content of Pousette-Dart's paintings relates them closely to the art of Mark Rothko and, to a lesser degree, Clyfford Still or Barnett Newman.

Peggy Guggenheim closed "Art of This Century" after its last show in May 1947. She had always preferred Europe to America and once the war was over decided to return, settling now in Venice and opening another museum-gallery of modern art. Before leaving New York, she did her best to place with other dealers the artists whom she had supported most enthusiastically. Pollock, of course, was her main concern since he was under contract. She approached several galleries, but most were reluctant to accept the artist because they were oriented more towards European than American modernism. At last, she was able to persuade Betty Parsons, who had opened a gallery in 1946, to give Pollock an exhibition and to represent him for the remainder of his contract. Parsons also represented Mark Rothko, Clyfford Still, Hans Hofmann and Richard Pousette-Dart in the late 1940s. Most of the other artists went to the Sam Kootz Gallery or to Marian Willard's.

No one today could dispute the fact that Peggy Guggenheim made an extremely important contribution to the development of contemporary American art through "Art of This Century". At a time when modern American painters and sculptors had little hope of showing their work and had only limited exposure to recent European trends, Peggy provided them with both and encouraged them to experiment on their own. "Art of This Century" was unique among the New York galleries. Critic Harold Rosenberg recognized this when he wrote:

"A relief from the past decade's WPA murals, Left Wing 'realism', and war agency posters, Peggy Guggenheim's war-time gallery was both old-fashioned and 'advanced'. It echoed the heroic days of Paris vanguardism of the twenties, and it evoked the tradition of individual experiment in twentieth-century art"[20].

It was a bridge between the past and present, where artists, critics and the public could measure the American avant-garde of the forties against the established European moderns, debating the relationships between them and assessing their qualitative and historical significance. It was, in short, a gallery dedicated to challenging the *status quo*, provoking discussion and illuminating the path of contemporary painting and sculpture. Peggy Guggenheim's desire that "Art of This Century" serve the future instead of recording the past was fulfilled – perhaps beyond what she had ever imagined possible.

Melvin P. Lader

Notes

1. Peggy Guggenheim, *Confessions of an Art Addict* (New York: Macmillan, 1960), p. 89.

2. "Peggy Guggenheim to Open Art Gallery – 'Art of This Century'", press release, October 1942, Peggy Guggenheim Archive, Palazzo Venier dei Leoni, Venice.

3. "Spring Salon for Young Artists", *The Nation* 156 (May 29, 1943): 786.

4. Press release, quoted in "Young Man From Wyoming", *Art Digest* 18 (November 1, 1943): 11.

5. James Johnson Sweeney, Foreword to *Jackson Pollock: Paintings and Drawings*, exhibition catalog, (New York: "Art of This Century", 1943), n.p.

6. Clement Greenberg, "Art", *The Nation* 157 (November 27, 1943): 621.

7. "Art of This Century" Accountant Reports, The Bernard and Rebecca Reis Papers, Archives of American Art, Smithsonian Institution, Washington, D.C.

8. Although no checklist or catalogue for Hofmann's exhibition at "Art of This Century" is known, the gouache in the Tel Aviv Museum dates from the time of the show and was a gift from Peggy Guggenheim to the Museum in 1954. In all probability, Guggenheim originally purchased the work from the exhibition for her own collection.

9. Newspaper clipping from the *Herald Tribune* dated March 26, 1944, in the Hans Hofmann artist file, New York Public Library.

10. "Baziotes has First One-Man Show at Peggy Guggenheim's 'Art of This Century'", press release, October 1944.

11. Clement Greenberg, "Art", *The Nation* 159 (November 11, 1944): 598.

12. Jon Stroup, "Motherwell Modern", *Art Digest* 19 (November 1, 1944): 16.

13. Maude Riley, "The Mythical Rothko and His Myths", *Art Digest* 19 (January 15, 1945): 15.

14. *Art News* 43 (January 15, 1945): 27.

15. Maude Riley, "Fifty-Seventh Street in Review", *Art Digest* 19 (November 15-30, 1944): 22.

16. Jon Stroup, Foreword to *Charles Seliger*, exhibition catalog (New York: "Art of This Century", 1945), n.p.

17. Clement Greenberg, "Art", *The Nation* 160 (April 7, 1945): 397.

18. Clement Greenberg "Art", *The Nation* 162 (February 9, 1946): 176.

19. *Richard Pousette Dart*, exhibition (New York: "Art of This Century", 1947), n.p.

20. Harold Rosenberg, "Collector as Creator", *Saturday Review* 43 (November 12, 1960): 30.

Exhibitions at "Art of This Century"

1942-1943 Season

Opening Exhibition: *Exhibition of the Collection*; October 20 - through November
Objects by Joseph Cornell; Marcel Duchamp's Box Valise; Laurence Vail Bottles; November 30 - through December
Exhibition by 31 Women: January 5 - 31
Retrospective Exhibition of the Works of Jean Hélion; February 8 - March 6
15 Early, 15 Late Paintings; March 13 - April 10
Exhibition of Collage; April 16 - May 15
Spring Salon for young Artists (under 35 years old); May 18 - June 26

1943-1944 Season

Masterworks of Early De Chirico; October 5 - November 6
First Exhibition: Jackson Pollock: Paintings and Drawings; November 9 - 27
Natural, Insane, Surrealist Art; November 30 - December 31
I. Rice Pereira; January 4 - 22
Arp; January 24 - February 29
Hans Hofmann; March 7 - 31
First Exhibition in America of (Twenty Paintings); April 11 - 30
Spring Salon for young Artists; May 2 - June 3
The Negro in American Life; May 29 - June 3

1944-1945 Season

Paintings and Drawings by William Baziotes: First One-Man Exhibition; October 3 - 21
Robert Motherwell: Paintings, Papiers Collés, Drawings; October 24 - November 11
Picasso Reproductions: Latest Works (1939-1943); October 24 - November 11
David Hare: Sculptures; November 14 - December 2
Rudolph Ray: Paintings; December 12 - January 6
Isabelle Waldberg: Constructions; December 12 - January 6
Christmas Suggestions; December 12 - January 6
Mark Rothko: Paintings; January 9 - February 4
Alberto Giacometti; February 10 - March 10
Laurence Vail; February 10 - March 10
Jackson Pollock; March 19 - April 14
Wolfgang Paalen; April 17 - May 12
Alice Rahon Paalen: Paintings; May 15 - June 7
The Women; June 12 - July 7

1945-1946 Season

Autumn Salon; October 6 - October (28?)
Charles Seliger: First Exhibition; October 30 - November 17
Paul Wilton; October 30 - November 17
Ted Bradley: Paintings; November 20 - December 8
Lee Hersch: Paintings; November 20 - December 8
Christmas Exhibition of Gouaches; December 11 - 29
Paintings by Janet Sobel; January 2 - 19
Sculpture by David Hare; January 22 - February 9
5 Sculptures: Pamela Bodin; February 12 - March 2
First Exhibition: Paintings: Clyfford Still; February 12 - March 2
Peter Busa: Paintings; March 9 - 30
Pegeen Vail: First Exhibition; March 9 - 30
Jackson Pollock: Exhibition: Paintings; April 2 - 20
Teresa Zarnower: 16 Gouaches; April 23 - May 11
Robert De Niro: First Exhibition of Painting; April 23 - May 11
Sonja Sekula: First Exhibition of Paintings; May 14 - June 1

1946-1947 Season

Hans Richter, 1919-1946; October 22 - November 9
Virginia Admiral; November 12 - 30
Rudi Blesh: Paintings 1946; November 12 - 30
Charles Seliger, Kenneth Scott, Dwight Ripley, John Goodwin, David Hill; December 3 - 21
Marjorie McKee; December 24 - January 11
Helen Schwinger; December 24 - January 11
Jackson Pollock; January 14 - February 1
Memorial Showing of the Last Paintings of Morris Hirshfield; February 1 - March 1
Richard Pousette-Dart; March 4 - 22
David Hare: Sculpture; March 25 - April 19
First American Retrospective Exhibition of Theo van Doesburg, 1883-1931; April 29 - May 31

Peggy Guggenheim in her
Venetian Palace.
Photograph courtesy
of the Estate of Roloff Beny.

Peggy Guggenheim's Donations

When the first truly public art collections were formed and when earlier royal collections were offered to the citizenry at large, pride in princely largesse was only one of the many and complex motivations. More significant was the firm and optimistic belief that art was one of the great teachers of mankind, and that the moral and spiritual well-being of the nation would be improved by contact with great paintings and sculptures that had until then been jealously guarded for the delight of a privileged few. It was also believed that public art collections would stimulate the imagination and energies of young artists, and improve the quality of craft and industry. But these hopes were not always fulfilled. Never, for instance, was the production of art at a lower level in Florence than in the decades following the Medici donation, to this day the most munificent public gift of art ever made. Yet these notions persisted throughout the nineteenth century and it is in their light that Peggy Guggenheim's activity as patron and donor can be viewed. Timing and her own fierce enthusiasm allowed her to succeed where so many well-intentioned eighteenth century princes had failed. Through her collecting and through her donations, Peggy Guggenheim exerted and continues to exert a strong didactic force. Though she played down her own intellectual prowess, she retained a bashful but unflagging respect for teaching, for learning, and for the innate will to refine and nourish the mind. Throughout her career her most ardent admiration went to her teachers: Emma Goldman, Sir Herbert Read, Marcel Duchamp, Alfred Barr and many others.

It was the instructive impulse that was behind the founding of her collection. From the first it was to have the double purpose of being an instrument of teaching as well as a means of financial and moral assistance to avant-garde artists. Throughout her life she distinguished mere acquaintances from real friends by the degree to which they realized that behind that cheerful flamboyance, behind the sophisticated hedonism of her ways, there was an energetic, purposeful mind at work bent on teaching. And on learning. It rarely happened that a friend suggested a stimulating book without her reading it as soon as possible. Of all the men and women of her social background, she was probably the most immune to boredom precisely because of her spontaneous need to learn and, in her way, to teach.

The teaching function of "Art of This Century", as has been pointed out in the preceding essay, consisted primarily in the presentation of exhibitions that were didactic because of the counterposing of works by the founding fathers of modern art with the work of still undiscovered talents. Often the installation of the exhibitions transformed the spectator, traditionally a passive element, into an active participant – thus driving home certain lessons by means of direct physical experience. For those of us who were growing up during the war years, the gallery was a recklessly liberal point of encounter and discussion. One never knew which artist would be arguing loudly with what other artist or critic. Although the younger visitors were too unprepared fully to understand these discussions, we did get the idea that contemporary and indeed all art was not simply to be enjoyed, respected, admired and studied. It could and *should* give rise to further adventures, to polemics, to the expression of still more, still newer ideas.

Within the framework of 57th Street during the forties, "Art of This Century" was unique. Within the framework of America coast-to-coast, 57th Street was unique. Where art and, especially, modern art was concerned, America was still a frontier country. On the East coast, with the exception of New York and New Haven, the number of works by twentieth century masters in public collections could be counted on the fingers of both hands (the Chester Dale Collection had not yet gone to Washington nor the Arensberg to Philadelphia). Looking westward, Cleveland, Detroit, Toledo and Cincinnati had made hesitant efforts but one had to go to Chicago to find a respectable concentration of fine paintings and sculptures by the pioneers of modern art. Between Chicago and San Francisco there was even less in the way of material which might challenge or surprise the incipient artist, art critic or art historian. Modern painting and sculptures were still suspect commodities. Even the WPA had done little to change attitudes. In the American hinterland, the word "artist" was almost automatically associated with the adjective "starving". The majority of the citizenry (and one must remember that the Great Depression was an overwhelming reality) felt that it was natural that artists should starve. Patriotic monuments might be considered a necessity for the nation's capital but urban sculptures or frescoes in post offices, even when they came from such well-trained but bland talents as Laredo Taft or Aaron Bohrod, were not accepted as essentials of civilization. Those museums that existed west of Chicago were primarily the creation of wealthy individuals who wanted to memorialize themselves and their fortunes by gifts of "safe" art, i.e. art of established and proven worth which could give pleasure, inspire awe or arouse intellectual curiosity. But by that very token it was an art incapable of bringing out the kind of passionately partisan debate that flared up in spontaneous combustion within the erratic setting of "Art of This Century".

It was with an eye towards extending this sort of excitement from 57th Street to the rest of America that Peggy Guggenheim acquired works by the artists of her "stable" to donate to what were then out-of-the-way museums. While most donors (Kress was the great exception) were interested in aggrandizing museums in their own cities, Peggy Guggenheim's campaign of donations was nation wide. In some cases, her gifts went to institutions which did not have a museum at all. Thus it was her gift of Jackson Pollock's most ambitious canvas as well as other important examples of contemporary American art that induced the administration of Iowa University to found one of the first State University museums in the Midwest. But it was not only relatively remote museums such as the Delgado Museum in New Orleans or the Seattle Museum of Art that were taken into consideration. Boston's Museum of Fine Arts had been in the forefront of acquiring contemporary art from its foundation to approximately the outbreak of the first World War. Then for reasons still unexplained by studies of art patronage, the museum's policies grew more conservative. In the hope of re-establishing Boston's impetus towards modern art, Perry Rathbone, a long-time friend of Peggy Guggenheim, turned to her for a donation and she responded generously. Later, impressed by the extraordinary enthusiasm for art in the newly-founded and embattled state of Israel, she made a major donation to the Tel Aviv Museum of Art and thus extended her benefits beyond the boundaries of America.

Peggy Guggenheim was less interested in appeals from European museums. In France and England there had been sufficient money and an infinite supply of works by local artists all through the twenties and thirties. She cannot be accused of chauvinism, as is evident from her memoirs and her life. But she was thrilled by the enthusiasm with which America welcomed the adventures and misadventures of modern art and felt that her support was more effective here than anywhere else. A twinge of pique may also have worked against her making gifts to European museums: only in the mid-fifties did European critics cease to ridicule her collection and her patronage.

It is almost impossible to assess the impact Peggy Guggenheim's donations made when they were received, just as it is impossible to tell what importance they will have in the future. Compared with her major gift – that of her private collection to The Solomon R. Guggenheim Foundation – the paintings and sculptures she bestowed on Boston, San Francisco or Raleigh seem scattered and somewhat lacking in consistency. But it is one thing for a young (or, for that matter, an old) art lover to be dazzled by the splendors of Palazzo Venier dei Leoni and quite another thing for that same art lover to be able to contemplate at leisure and repeatedly a Pollock or a Matta or a Clyfford Still in his own home town. There is a sense of communality, a more intimate connection that can, under the right circumstances, make a superb Hélion in Raleigh, an Alan Davie in Providence or a Nicholson in Tel Aviv more fruitful than a whole roomful of Picassos encountered during hasty travels. The effect art has on mind and emotion is one of the great imponderables. The important thing is to take the risk of bringing artist and public together. The risk is very real when both artist and public are one's contemporaries because there is no guarantee that the artist is worthy of the public just as there is no guarantee that the public is worthy of the artist. Peggy Guggenheim, at the height of her career, thrived on risks and, following her instincts, staked what she had on the quality of the artist whose work she wanted to support and on the enthusiasm of a public that was totally unknown to her. It takes an act of imagination to estimate the significance of Peggy Guggenheim's gifts of art made nearly fifty years ago. Unlike the gift of, say, a Ruijsdael or a Fra Angelico, each painting and sculpture that she donated represented a challenge to the audience. The museum staff and the trustees had to ask themselves, "Is this art worth having?". The museum visitor had to ask himself, "is this art related to the needs and hopes of my existence? Can I decipher it? Can I make it mine?". For there existed as yet no authority, no respected body of interpretations to which one could have recourse.

The import of Peggy Guggenheim's gifts is well summed up by Dr. Franklin Robinson, Director of the Museum of Art at the Rhode Island School of Design:

"... the lasting effect of Ms. Guggenheim's donation was simply to pull us into the Post-War period, to make us aware of and excited about, the art of the forties and fifties in this country and abroad. The Jackson Pollock is, quite simply, the most important painting by a twentieth century American in our collection, and it will always be one of the great glories of this Museum".

Similarly, the Curator of the Tel Aviv Museum, Dr. Nehama Guralnik states:

"At the time the donation was made by Peggy Guggenheim, in the early fifties, the Tel Aviv Museum lacked any representation of American art, and included a limited representation of abstract and Surrealist art. During the following years, the donation served as a catalyst for the enlargement of the collection in both these categories.

Furthermore, the donation formed the core of an exhibition entitled *Abstract and Surrealist Art* which opened in January 1955, and which was visited by some 50,000 people. The exhibition presented international modernism to the local public for the first time and was the most important and influential exhibition of modern art that had taken place in Israel during the first decade of its existence. It brought about donations of important works by several of the participating artists (among them Max Ernst's *Bewildered Planet* of 1942 and Jean Arp's *Four White Shapes Constellating on a Blue Background* of 1953)".

The spirit and the humor behind Peggy Guggenheim's donations are clearly expressed by the following excerpt from the Northwest Oral History Project (Archives of American Art, Smithsonian Institution, 1983):

"When Edward B. Thomas (Curator of the Seattle Art Museum) visited Venice in 1954 he arranged a meeting with Guggenheim and the two hit it off immediately. Thomas' visit coincided with a rather pompous visitor who was reviewing works for purchase. Reacting to the other visitor's attitude Guggenheim turned to me in a stage whisper and said, 'stick around, honey, and I'll give you one'. When the other guest had gone, she said, 'Okay, let's go down to the basement; I have five Jackson Pollocks set up and you can have your pick of any of them'.

At the time the Guggenheim gifts entered our collection, the museum was noted primarily for its Asian and regional holdings, and the gift helped to underline the need to expand the museum's modern holdings. Both the quality of the gifts and the prestige of the giver have helped the Seattle Art Museum to establish its modern art collection and have interestingly provided an excellent inducement to other collectors to become involved in the museum".

That there were some donations of lesser quality is not as surprising as is the small number of "mistakes". Nor were the less felicitous donations always due to Peggy Guggenheim's choice. More than one museum director has confessed, under the seal of collegial discretion, that he had made something of a gaffe by choosing an object that turned out to be less significant than several alternatives offered by Peggy Guggenheim. Wisdom of hindsight, though it is a pleasant pastime, should never be taken too seriously. The museum directors took risks and so did Peggy; both should be honored for it. That the preponderant majority of these risks paid off handsomely cannot be attributed to good luck. Neither patron nor beneficiary were playing roulette. Peggy wanted to teach; at the same time she also wanted to learn. With great shrewdness and perception she chose her professors and then did a great deal of homework on her own.

There was another element that must not be undervalued. Giving can be fun and for many years she enjoyed seeing museum directors, especially those who had become close friends, walk away with their trophies. Exactly when and why the fun began to pall is difficult to determine but slowly her involvement in the art world as a whole began to slacken. No one will ever know why Peggy Guggenheim decided to close "Art of This Century" and retreat from center-front stage of the art world, a retreat which accelerated visibly after the mid-fifties. In spite of the statements she made in print, her motivations were far from clear to herself. Like all fundamental human choices, the reasons for her move to Venice are probably too complex and too contradictory to be resolved by documentary evidence. She may have felt in some obscure way that she had accomplished what she set out to do. Along with a few select colleagues such as Alfred Barr, she had been instrumental in rallying vast sectors of the public to the cause of contemporary art. In fact, she felt in her later years that she had won her battle rather too thoroughly. She began to see that art was in danger of being loved to death, particularly in America. Her flair, her enthusiasm and her commitment had made modern art a prime concern, almost a tacit obligation. The sense of risk, the feeling of coming to grips with forces that would become recognizable only in the future, had gone. So overwhelming has now the interest in art become that the most influential and financially unbeatable powers in the world of art education have issued statements equating a lack of interest with a state of sub-human existence - as if Mother Theresa were to be looked on askance because she knows not of and cares not for Larry Poons or Carl André. Though Peggy Guggenheim had been part of the exuberant free-for-all which had propagated awareness of the avant-garde and its central place in contemporary civilization, she felt increasingly that the time had come for a more thoughtful (not necessarily more pedantic or academic) reassessment of modern art. She grew more and more detached from the immediate present and devoted herself more to the care and exhibition of her collection. Her interest in helping museums diminished; rather than giving works of art away, she thought of rounding out what she had already acquired. Her last serious negotiations before advancing age and illness overtook her, concerned the acquisition, unfortunately thwarted, of a painting by Philip Guston.

A decade or so ago, on a rainy Venetian autumn afternoon, Peggy was desultorily going through old letters and ledgers left over from the forties and fifties. I had recently visited San Francisco and told her how excited I had been to see a superb Theo van Doesburg in the local Museum of Modern Art labelled "Gift of Peggy Guggenheim". She was pleased and began recalling other donations she had made. It occurred to me then that the re-assembling of the works she had scattered far and wide would make a good exhibition for any museum interested in the manifold aspects of taste and patronage during a crucial period of American art. At first she was delighted by the idea; the possibility appealed to her of seeing again paintings and sculptures she had once owned. Then, quite suddenly her mood sank.

"People will say that I must have been a fool to give such things away".

She sounded neither bitter nor resigned. She knew the world because she had been a part of it herself. Since then, much has been written about Peggy Guggenheim and she has been described in terms of endearment, in terms of reproach and in terms of dry historical fact. But nobody has implied that she was a fool – with the single exception of Bernard Berenson, who, after visiting her collection at the 1948 Venice Biennale, turned to her: "You should have come to me, my dear, I would have found you bargains".

Fred Licht

Public museums that received donations from Peggy Guggenheim:

Atlanta, Georgia	High Museum of Art
Boston, Massachusetts	Museum of Fine Arts
Chicago, Illinois	Art Institute of Chicago
Hartford, Connecticut	Wadsworth Atheneum
Iowa City, Iowa	University of Iowa Museum of Art
Kansas City, Missouri	Nelson Atkins Museum of Art
New York, New York	Brooklyn Museum
New York, New York	Museum of Modern Art
New Haven, Connecticut	Yale University Art Gallery
New Orleans, Louisiana	New Orleans Museum of Art
Phoenix, Arizona	Phoenix Art Museum
Poughkeepsie, New York	Vassar College Art Gallery
Providence, Rhode Island	Museum of the Rhode Island School of Design
Raleigh, North Carolina	North Carolina Museum of Art
San Diego, California	San Diego Museum of Art
San Francisco, California	San Francisco Museum of Modern Art
Seattle, Washington	Seattle Art Museum
Tel Aviv, Israel	The Tel Aviv Museum

Catalogue

Jean Arp
1. **Collage No. 3 in Glass.** 1964
   Glass, 19 ⅝ x 25 ½"
   Collection The Phoenix Art Museum,
   Gift of Peggy Guggenheim.

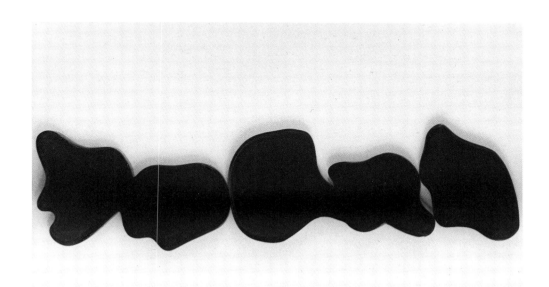

Jean Arp
2. **Nude.** 1964
Glass, 10 ⅛ x 13 ⅜ x 5"
Collection Museum of Fine Arts, Boston,
Gift of Peggy Guggenheim.

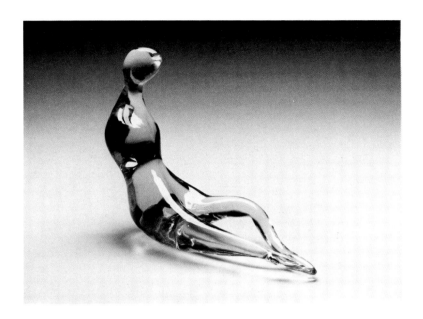

Jean Arp
3.   **La Colomba.** 1964 (?)
Glass, 10 ¼ x 9 ⅝ x 5 ⁵⁄₁₆"
Collection Museum of Fine Arts, Boston,
Gift of Peggy Guggenheim.

William Baziotes
4. **The Mirror at Midnight I.** ca. 1942
    Oil on canvas, 12 x 16"
    Private Collection.

William Baziotes

5. **The Drugged Balloonist.** ca. 1942-1943
Collage on paperboard, 18 ¼ x 24"
Collection The Baltimore Museum of Art,
Bequest of Saidie A. May (BMA 1951.266).

William Baziotes
6. **The Boudoir.** 1944
Oil on canvas, 34 ½ x 50"
Private Collection.

William Baziotes
7. **The Parachutists.** 1944
Duco enamel on canvas, 30 x 40"
Collection Ethel Baziotes, New York,
courtesy Blum Helman Gallery,
New York.

William Baziotes
8. **The Hour Glass.** ca. 1944
Oil on canvas, 30 x 24"
Collection Mr. and Mrs. Meredith Long, Houston.

Collective Drawing
9. **Fantastic Birds.** 1940
    Crayon and ink on paper, 12 ½ x 16 ⅝6"
    Collection Tel Aviv Museum,
    Gift of Peggy Guggenheim.

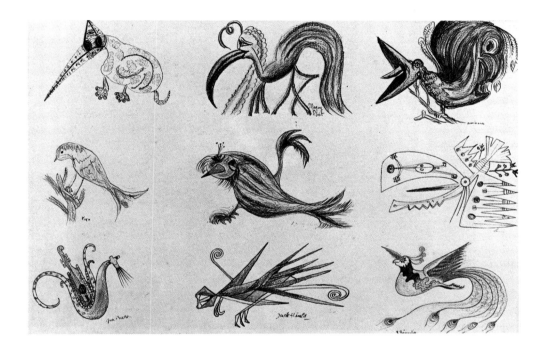

Pietro Consagra
10. **Untitled.** 1948
Iron, 83 x 16 x 16"
Collection New Orleans Museum of Art,
Gift of Peggy Guggenheim.

Theo van Doesburg
11. **Simultaneous Counter Composition.** 1929
Oil on canvas, 19 ¾ x 19 ¾"
Collection San Francisco Museum of Modern Art,
Gift of Peggy Guggenheim.

Max Ernst
12. **The Numerous Family.** 1926
Oil on canvas, 32 ⅛ x 25 ⅜"
Collection San Francisco Museum of Modern Art,
Gift of Peggy Guggenheim.

Max Ernst
13.   **Bauta.** 1964
Glass, 19 ⅝ x 9 ¾ x 11"
Collection San Francisco Museum of Modern Art,
Gift of Peggy Guggenheim.

Max Ernst
14. **Bird.** 1964
Glass, 15 ⅜ x 9 ¼ x 2 ¾"
Collection Museum of Fine Arts, Boston,
Gift of Peggy Guggenheim.

Claire Falkenstein
15. **Gate (Model for Palazzo Venier).** 1963
Soldered iron wire and glass, 17 ⅛ x 14 ½ x 1"
Collection Museum of Fine Arts, Boston,
Gift of Peggy Guggenheim.

Otto Freundlich
16. **Geometric Abstraction.** 1938
Gouache on paper, 41 x 28"
Collection Seattle Art Museum,
Gift of Peggy Guggenheim.

42

David Hare
17. **Dead Elephant.** 1945
Sorel cement, 4 ⅜ x 11 ⅜ x 6 ¼"
Collection San Francisco Museum of Modern Art,
Gift of Jeanne Reynal.

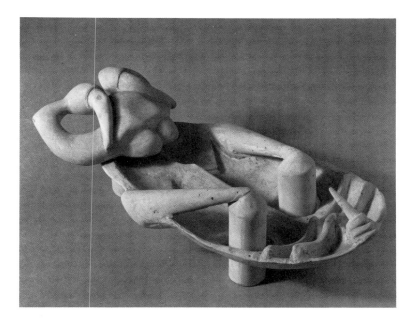

David Hare
18. **The Couple.** 1946
Cement, 61 ½ x 17 x 13"
Courtesy Gruenebaum Gallery, New York.

Jean Hélion
19. **Untitled.** 1934
Oil on canvas, 51 x 64"
Collection North Carolina Museum of Art, Raleigh,
Gift of Peggy Guggenheim.

Morris Hirshfield
20. **Stage Beauties.** 1944
Oil on canvas, 40 x 48"
Courtesy Sidney Janis Gallery, New York.

46

Morris Hirshfield
21. **Nude with Flowers.** 1945
Oil on canvas, 26 ¾ x 21 ¾"
Courtesy Sidney Janis Gallery, New York.

Hans Hofmann
22. **Untitled.** ca. 1943
Gouache and pencil on paper, 19 ½ x 26 ¼"
Collection Tel Aviv Museum,
Gift of Peggy Guggenheim.

Gerome Kamrowski
23. **Untitled.** 1942
Oil on canvas, 19 x 20"
Collection of the artist.

Willem de Kooning
24. **The Wave.** ca. 1942-1944
Oil on fiberboard, 48 x 48"
Collection National Museum of American Art,
Smithsonian Institution, Washington, D.C.,
Gift from the Vincent Melzac Collection.

50

André Masson
25. **The Ride.** 1927
Oil on canvas, 24 x 14 ³⁄₁₆”
Collection Tel Aviv Museum,
Gift of Peggy Guggenheim.

Matta
26. **Like Me, Like X.** 1942
Oil on canvas, 28 x 36"
Collection The University of Iowa Museum of Art,
Iowa City,
Gift of Peggy Guggenheim.

Matta
27.   **Abstraction.** n.d.
Oil on paper, 57 x 74 ½"
Collection Museum of Art, Rhode Island School of Design,
Providence,
Gift of Peggy Guggenheim.

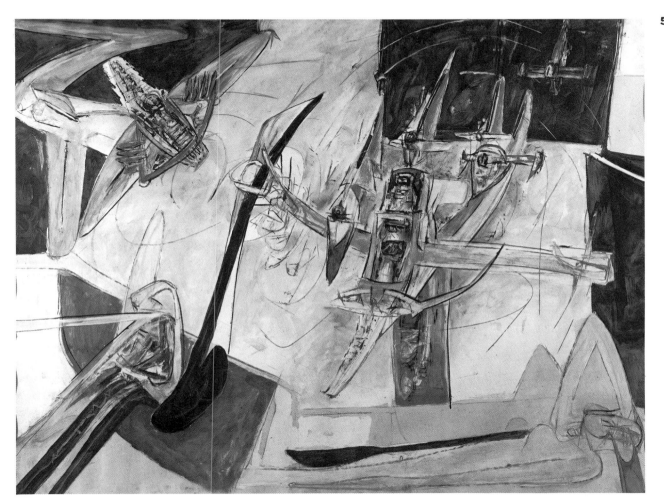

Robert Motherwell
28. **The Little Spanish Prison.** 1941-1944
Oil on canvas, 27 ¼ x 17 ⅛"
Collection The Museum of Modern Art, New York,
Gift of Renate Ponsold Motherwell.

Robert Motherwell
29. **Pancho Villa, Dead and Alive.** 1943
Gouache and oil with collage on cardboard, 28 x 35 ⅞"
Collection The Museum of Modern Art, New York,
Purchase.

Robert Motherwell
30. **Personage.** 1943
Oil on canvas, 48 x 38"
Collection Norton Gallery of Art, West Palm Beach,
Florida.

Robert Motherwell
31. **The Door (Mexico).** 1943
Ink and watercolor on paper mounted on board, 13 ¼ x 10"
Collection Thomas Marc Futter.

Robert Motherwell
32. **The Displaced Table.** 1943
    Oil on canvas, 41 x 30"
    Private Collection.
    [Not in exhibition]

Irene Rice Pereira
33. **Eight Oblongs.** 1943
Encaustic on parchment, 19 x 25"
Collection The University of Iowa Museum of Art,
Iowa City,
Gift of Peggy Guggenheim.

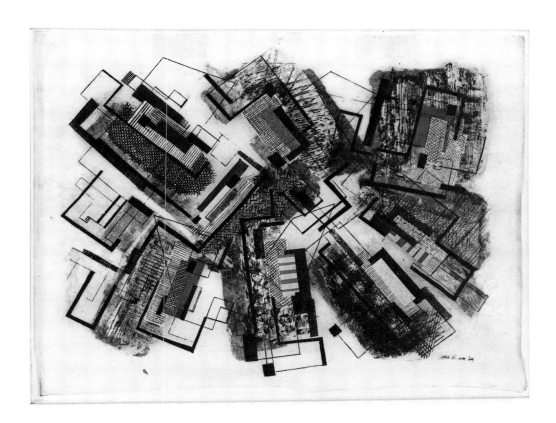

Pablo Picasso
34. **Centaur.** ca. 1965
Glass with pigment, 12 ¼ x 3 ⅞ x 11 ½"
Collection San Francisco Museum of Modern Art,
Gift of Peggy Guggenheim.

Jackson Pollock
35. **Burning Landscape.** 1943
Oil and gesso on canvas, 36 x 28 ⁷⁄₁₆"
Yale University Art Gallery, New Haven,
Gift of Peggy Guggenheim.

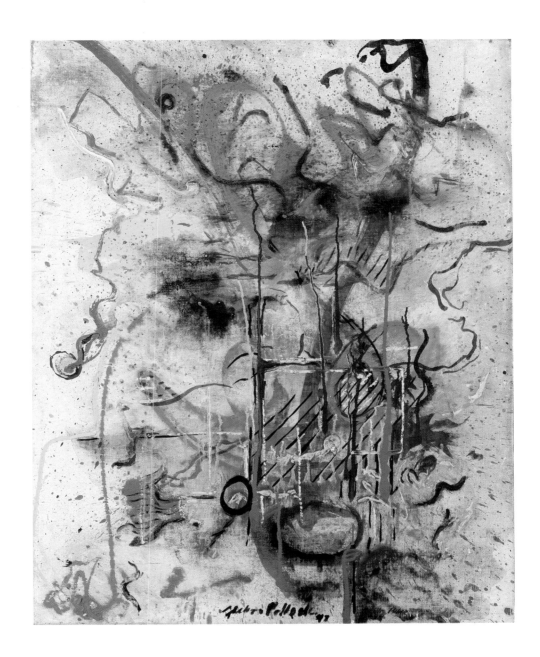

Jackson Pollock

36. **The She-Wolf.** 1943
Oil, gouache and plaster on canvas, 41 ⅞ x 67"
Collection The Museum of Modern Art, New York,
Purchase.

Jackson Pollock
37. **Mural.** 1943
Oil on canvas, 97 ¼ x 238"
Collection The University of Iowa Museum of Art,
Iowa City,
Gift of Peggy Guggenheim.

Jackson Pollock
38. **Portrait of H.M.** 1945
Oil on canvas, 36 x 43"
Collection The University of Iowa Museum of Art,
Iowa City,
Gift of Peggy Guggenheim.

Jackson Pollock

39. **There Were Seven in Eight.** ca. 1945
Oil on canvas, 43 x 101"
Collection The Museum of Modern Art, New York,
Mr. and Mrs. Walter Bareiss Fund and Purchase.

Jackson Pollock
40. **Shimmering Substance.** 1946
Oil on canvas, 30 ⅛ x 24 ¼"
From the Sounds in the Grass Series
Collection The Museum of Modern Art, New York, Mr. and
Mrs. Albert Lewin and Mrs. Sam A. Lewisohn Funds.

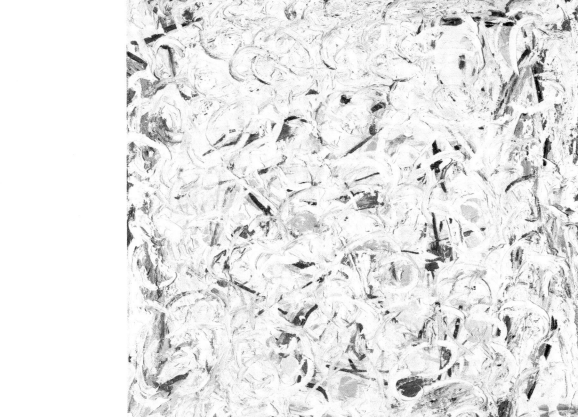

Jackson Pollock
41. **Full Fathom Five.** 1947
Oil on canvas with nails, tacks, buttons, keys, coins,
cigarettes, matches, etc., 50 ⅞ x 30 ⅛"
Collection The Museum of Modern Art, New York,
Gift of Peggy Guggenheim.

Jackson Pollock
42. **Magic Lantern.** 1947
Oil, metallic paint and nails on canvas, 42 ⅞ x 21 ¾"
Collection Museum of Art, Rhode Island School of Design,
Providence, Gift of Peggy Guggenheim.

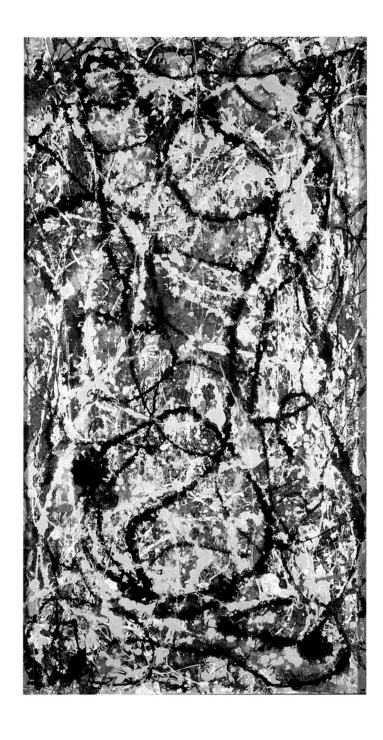

Richard Pousette-Dart
43. **Portrait of Pegeen.** 1940-1942
     Oil on canvas, 50 x 52"
     Private Collection.

Richard Pousette-Dart
44. **Symphony No. 1, The Transcendental.** 1942
Oil on canvas, 85 ½ x 139 ¼"
Private Collection.

Richard Pousette-Dart
45. **Figure.** 1943-1945
Oil on canvas, 79 ⅞ x 50"
Private Collection.

Richard Pousette-Dart
46. **Undulation.** 1943-1945
Oil on canvas, 48 x 93 ⅝"
Private Collection.

Richard Pousette-Dart
47. **Comprehension of the Atom, Crucifixion.** ca. 1944
     Oil on canvas, 77 ⅝ x 49 ⅛"
     Private Collection.

Mark Rothko
48. **Gyration on Four Planes.** 1944
Oil on canvas, 24 ¼ x 48 ⅛"
Collection Philadelphia Museum of Art,
Gift of The Mark Rothko Foundation, Inc.

74

Mark Rothko
49. **Poised Elements.** 1944
Oil on canvas, 36 x 47 ¾"
Collection Mr. and Mrs. Edward J. Minskoff, New York.

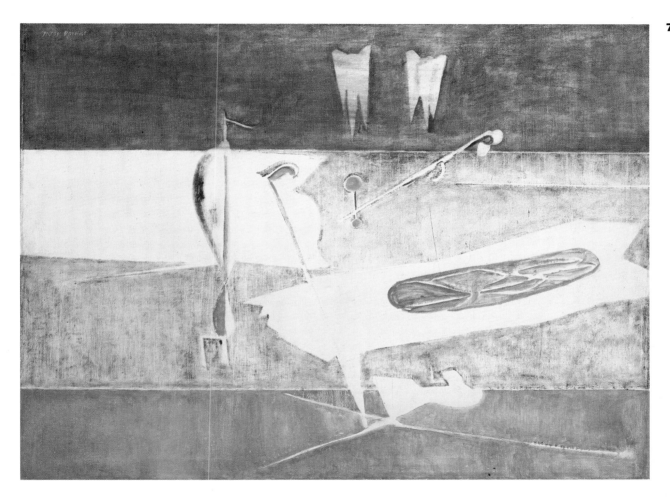

Mark Rothko
50. **Ritual.** 1944
Oil and pencil on canvas, 53 $^{15}/_{16}$ x 39 ½"
Collection Walker Art Center, Minneapolis,
Gift of The Mark Rothko Foundation, Inc., 1986.

Mark Rothko
51. **Slow Swirl by the Edge of the Sea.** 1944
Oil on canvas, 75 ⅜ x 84 ¾"
Collection The Museum of Modern Art, New York,
Bequest of Mrs. Mark Rothko through The Mark Rothko
Foundation, Inc.

Mark Rothko
52. **Hierarchical Birds.** 1944
Oil on canvas, 39 ⅝ x 31 ⅝"
Collection National Gallery of Art, Washington, D.C.,
Gift of The Mark Rothko Foundation, Inc.

Charles Seliger
53. **Cerebral Landscape.** 1944
Oil on canvas, 24 3/16 x 18 3/16"
Collection Wadsworth Atheneum, Hartford,
Gift of Mr. and Mrs. Alexis Zalstem-Zalessky.

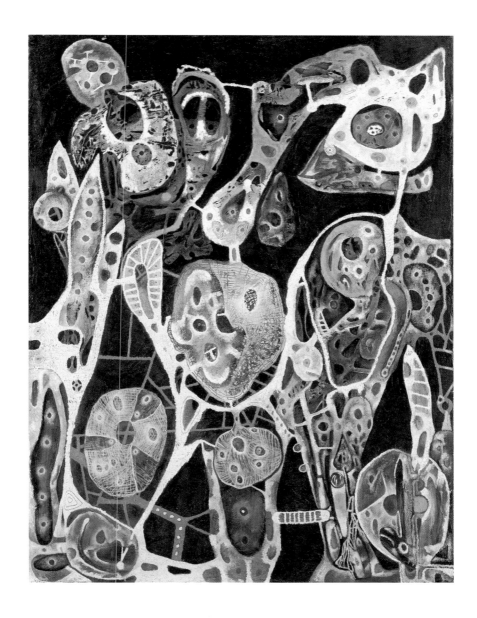

Charles Seliger
54.   **Don Quixote.** 1944
Oil on canvas, 30 x 40"
Collection Elaine and Hyman G. Weitzen.

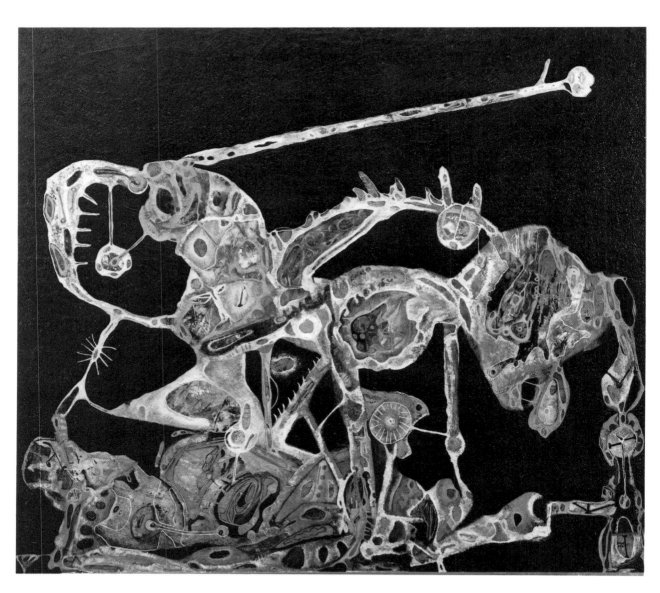

Charles Seliger
55. **The Last Cyclops.** 1945
Oil on canvas, 22 x 22"
Collection of the artist.

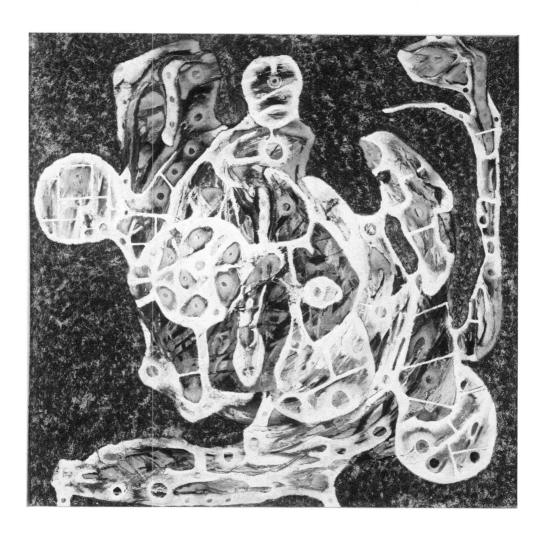

Janet Sobel
56. **Milky Way.** 1945
Enamel on canvas, 44 ⅞ x 29 ⅞"
Collection The Museum of Modern Art, New York,
Gift of the artist's family.

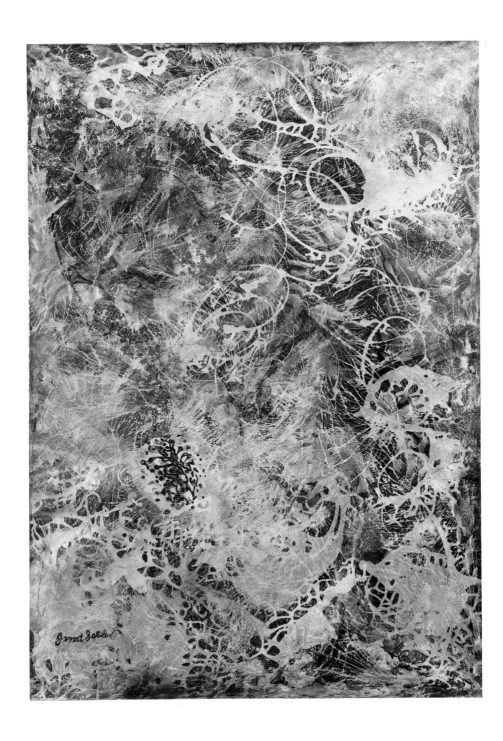

Laurence Vail
57. **Perfect Lady.** 1942
Glass bottle assemblage, 14" high
Collection Daniel Rosenblatt, New York.

Laurence Vail
58. **Madame Bovary.** 1943
Glass bottle assemblage, 14 ½" high
Collection Timothy Baum, New York.

Lenders to the Exhibition

Timothy Baum, New York
Ethel Baziotes
Thomas Marc Futter
Gerome Kamrowski
Mr. and Mrs. Meredith Long, Houston
Mr. and Mrs. Edward J. Minskoff, New York
Daniel Rosenblatt, New York
Charles Seliger
Mr. and Mrs. Hyman G. Weitzen

The Baltimore Museum of Art
Museum of Art, Rhode Island School of Design, Providence
Museum of Fine Arts, Boston
The Museum of Modern Art, New York
National Gallery of Art, Washington, D.C.
National Museum of American Art, Smithsonian Institution,
Washington, D.C.
New Orleans Museum of Art
North Carolina Museum of Art, Raleigh
Norton Gallery of Art, West Palm Beach, Florida
Philadelphia Museum of Art
The Phoenix Art Museum
San Francisco Museum of Modern Art
Seattle Art Museum
Tel Aviv Museum
University of Iowa Museum of Art, Iowa City
Wadsworth Atheneum, Hartford
Walker Art Center, Minneapolis
Yale University Art Gallery, New Haven

Blum Helman Gallery, New York
Gruenebaum Gallery, New York
Sidney Janis Gallery, New York

The New York exhibition of "Peggy Guggenheim's Other Legacy" is made possible by a generous grant from **The Bankers Trust Company Group.**

The Solomon R. Guggenheim Foundation is grateful to the **Regione Veneto** for the annual subsidy that assures the effective operation of the Peggy Guggenheim Collection, Venice.

The extended season of the Peggy Guggenheim Collection is made possible through a grant from **United Technologies Corporation.**

The free Saturday evening opening of the Peggy Guggenheim Collection is financed by a grant from **Montedison Progetto Cultura.**

The Solomon R. Guggenheim Foundation gratefully acknowledges the support of **Alitalia** on an annual basis.

Photographic Credits

This volume was printed
in February 1987 by F. Ghezzi
for Arnoldo Mondadori Editore
for the Trustees of The Solomon
R. Guggenheim Foundation.
Printed in Italy.